Using assessment to raise achievement in mathematics at key stages 1, 2 and 3

Supporting *Assessment for Learning*

Evidence suggests that using good strategies for formative assessment could lead to significant improvements in the performance of pupils. This guidance aims to provide information about using the following techniques:

- involving pupils in assessing their own performance (section 1);
- setting learning goals for pupils and sharing these with them (section 1);
- using effective questioning techniques to assess and further pupils' learning (section 2);
- using marking and feedback strategies to inform pupils about their progress (section 3).

This guidance considers each of these aspects and illustrates how some schools have used them.

Contents

Introduction

> Where anyone is trying to learn, feedback about their efforts has three elements – *the desired goal*, the evidence about their *present position*, and some understanding of *a way to close the gap* between the two.
>
> [Sadler, 1989]

This guidance has been inspired by the documents *Inside the black box* (Black & Wiliam, 1998) and *Assessment for Learning, Beyond the black box* (Assessment Reform Group, 1999). *Inside the black box* showed that standards are raised by concentrating on formative assessment. The study posed three questions: is there evidence that improving formative assessment raises standards?; is there evidence that there is room for improvement in the practice of assessment?; and is there evidence about how to improve formative assessment? This research evidence pointed to an unqualified 'yes' as the answer to each of these questions.

Quantitative evidence suggests that, through good strategies for formative assessment, improvement equivalent to an average of two grades at GCSE can be achieved. Some of this evidence suggests that if England had been employing these 'good strategies' in assessment, the country would have been ranked in the top 5 of the 41 countries involved in the Third International Mathematics and Science Study 1995, instead of its position in the middle of the ranking.

Inside the black box also reveals that there is considerable room for improvement in assessment strategies. It suggests that some strategies encourage rote and superficial learning, that they frequently have a negative impact and that strategies are often used as a management tool, not as a system to discern learning needs.

This guidance seeks to analyse and illuminate some of the issues associated with *assessment for learning* (sometimes referred to as formative assessment). Within these pages, learning is sometimes portrayed as the process of closing the gap between the current knowledge, skills and understanding of pupils and the planned desired learning goals (Sadler, 1989). The extent of the gap is determined through self-assessment – this establishes the current position of the pupils' knowledge – and by sharing the desired learning objectives with pupils. The gap is closed through questioning and through identifying how teaching might respond to pupils' work and how teachers can use their knowledge of pupils' common mistakes and misconceptions.

At the end of section 3 case studies are used to illustrate how schools have implemented aspects of this work.

Section 1: Learning goals, self-assessment and peer assessment

Effective learning will occur only if pupils are clear about what they know, understand and can do at the start of a piece of work and what they will know, understand and be able to do when they have completed the work.

The first part of this section highlights how self-assessment helps pupils to become effective learners by enabling them to reflect on:

- their knowledge of themselves as thinkers and learners;
- their understanding of the task in hand;
- their tactical knowledge of how to improve their own learning.

Peer assessment is useful because pupils can:

- develop new strategies by scrutinising the work of others;
- become more efficient in using assessment criteria.

The second part of this section draws on recent studies and research to illustrate how important and effective it is to set and share learning goals with pupils. We might use the analogy of 'signposting' to describe this. If we are on a journey we need to be clear about where we are going. Signposts that tell us we are still going in the right direction and that we are getting closer will help us to feel confident. A signpost that shows us we are getting further away from our destination is also valuable as we will stop, check and try to get back on the right road.

Self-assessment

If learning is to be efficient, pupils must be active agents in judging the gap between what they know and what they need to know. This implies that learning will be more effective if the pupil practises self-assessment because this will make them aware of their level of understanding. The teacher can then help them to close the gap by sharing learning goals with them. However, only the pupil can do the actual learning. The issue of shared learning goals is addressed later in this section.

Assessment for learning can be used to help the pupil to become an effective learner, not only through better study techniques but also by developing the capacity for being aware of what they know, understand and can do. Therefore pupils need to achieve a strategic overview of the learning task and to understand their own status and role in relation to that task.

If pupils are to become increasingly responsible for their own learning then they must also be involved in their own assessment. This is most effective if the work is structured to contain shared learning goals, thus pupils can monitor their learning on a continuous basis.

Many pupils have been shown to lack a clear overview of their learning and have become confused because they do not understand the criteria on which to base their own assessments. In many classrooms, pupils do not perceive the structure of the learning aims that give meaning to their work. Therefore they are unable to assess their own progress.

Self-assessment requires a reflective judgement of one's own work; the capacity to make such judgements is an essential feature of effective learning.

Self-assessment exercise: traffic lights

In a school in Kent all pupils take a test in mathematics each half-term. After the test one teacher proceeds as follows. All the students look through their tests and think about where and why they have made mistakes. They use a code, which they call *traffic lights*, to record their understanding of each topic and subtopic. If they have full marks in part of the test and feel confident about this topic they put a green blob on a record of attainment specifically designed for this. However, they might have full marks and place an amber blob if they feel that was a fluke. They might have almost full marks and put a green blob if they feel they had made a silly mistake that could be easily avoided next time. If they score almost nothing on a particular topic they almost certainly use a red blob although, again, they might judge that amber was more appropriate.

After this self-assessment exercise the teacher collects records of attainment and looks through them. If topics have red blobs from most of the pupils the teacher knows to go over that topic again. Many topics will have an assortment of different coloured blobs against them and the teacher will ask the pupils to prioritise the topics in their own learning agenda.

Peer assessment

The purpose of pupils comparing themselves with their peers is to help the pupils to move forward. It is not for the purpose of ranking because if pupils compare themselves with others rather than their own previous attainment, those with high attainments are little challenged and those with low attainments are demotivated.

In one school a homework exercise was set requiring pupils to write an explanation of Pythagoras' Theorem followed by an account of how to use it. When this was complete a peer marked the work. The peer needed to consider:

- Does the explanation make sense?
- Is it complete?
- Are the examples clear?

This assessment process helped the marker to make progress because they had to crystalise their own thinking.

Peer assessment can also add to effective learning because it provides pupils with evidence to use in comparison with their own work. It gives pupils both a wider view of what is possible and encouragement to reflect on the task and what it means to accomplish the learning aims.

All of this can occur without the complication of pupils feeling intellectually threatened. Research shows that improving skills in self-assessment and peer assessment is necessary to accomplish other developments essential to effective learning. These include:

- greater personal responsibility;
- more reflection on one's learning;
- enhanced self-esteem and motivation.

Setting learning goals

Target-setting is an integral part of the teaching and learning process: teachers, in their day-to-day work, will have numerous discussions with pupils about what they have done, what they are doing and what they might need to do next. This section looks at targets from a different perspective to that found in much recent writing, where they are often phrased in terms of national curriculum levels. What we try to do here is look at how pupils' learning can be enhanced if they work towards specific learning targets that they can relate to.

An important feature of setting targets relating to academic progress has been not only to focus on a specific aspect of learning but also to describe the criteria for success. If pupils are to be effective learners they need to be able to evaluate their progress against criteria they can understand.

Target-setting

Some schools use quite formal methods of recording half-termly targets and reviewing them regularly. Others make strong links between target-setting and marking. Targets may, for instance, be listed inside the cover of a pupil's book and explicitly referred to when the teacher marks pieces of work. This marking is reviewed with the pupil. Finding time for regular review with pupils is a major issue if targets are to be meaningful for pupils.

Some of the difficulties inherent in more traditional target-setting can be seen in comments from teachers in the Medway and Oxfordshire project run with Kings' College London (Black & Wiliam, 2000). Teachers often resorted to bland and rather meaningless statements such as 'do better' or 'concentrate harder'. This can arise when national curriculum levels are the sole focus for pupils and so targets are considered too distant or large for pupils to get to grips with. Bringing targets down to the classroom level and to achievable and understandable statements is therefore important.

One teacher gave pupils sheets to put in their books so they could record their targets and have time at the start of each lesson to think about them. At the end of the lesson the teacher asked pupils to think about what they had achieved towards meeting their targets and to set themselves a target for the next lesson, which they wrote in their books.

Another teacher used a sheet with a column for pupils to make their own response. Many pupils used this to record when they had met their targets or to respond to the teacher's comments.

Learning-related targets

In interviews with children as part of the LEARN project it became clear that pupils found explicit learning-related targets useful, as can be seen by the following comments:

> Yes, we have them hanging up and we set targets with our teacher. It is helpful. I usually forget paragraphs and the target reminds me. (Year 6)

> I look at the target and it reminds me what to do. When you finish a target you are allowed to do a picture. (Year 6)

> Some teachers write targets on your report. That's useful 'cos you can work to it. (Year 9)

> We have to set ourselves targets coursework-wise. The teachers give us advice on how to set these targets. (Year 11)

The project also found that targets were sometimes something of a formality – they were set when reports were written but rarely followed up:

> We have three targets set at parents' evening. (Year 3)

> In our organisers we've got a special page for targets. I've only ever done it once I think. Basically we don't get told to do it. (Year 9)

> I think we have targets. I can't remember where they came from. (Year 9)

> In our reports they set us targets. I probably won't look back at them myself but we might in a lesson. (Year 10)

> We write targets in our planner – I never look at them. (Year 10)

Making learning goals understandable

In a school in Birmingham, four teachers of year 7 mathematics classes have started to look at the effects of explicitly encouraging children to think about their task as that of 'becoming a mathematician'. This is translated into activities such as asking questions, trying things out, looking for connections and asking why. This makes explicit to the pupils what constitutes mathematical activity and moderates the image of mathematics as a subject with lots of rules to learn. Pupils, when asked what they have learned, often make statements about these features of becoming mathematicians as well as statements about the specific content they have been working on. They are thus showing that they can understand bigger goals and aims, and look further forward in their learning.

Addressing misconceptions

A review of recent research in mathematics education (Ofsted, 1995, pp12-13) discussed research into the effectiveness of explicitly addressing, exposing and discussing misconceptions in teaching. All pupils acquire a range of ideas during their learning of mathematics, which can lead them to misunderstandings. A common example would be the use of the 'rule' that to multiply by 10 they add a zero. If a pupil does not understand the features of place value they can find their 'rule' lets them down when they apply it to decimals. This misconception then needs to be directly exposed and discussed in order for pupils to understand why their previous understanding is no longer adequate. This implies that the learning goals for this part of mathematics should be explicit and openly addressed.

The effect of mentoring on the academic achievement of boys

A recent research project in Northampton looked at the effectiveness of mentoring on boys' achievement (Mitchell & Hirom, 1999). It also had some points to make about the value of pupils understanding the aims and objectives of their study.
One-to-one mentoring sessions provided a forum for pupils to explore their understanding of the expectations their teachers had of them. This enabled them to clarify the learning goals that were important for them in developing autonomy as learners.

The teacher's role in pupils' self-assessment

The teacher's role in pupils' self-assessment is to help the pupils understand what it is they are trying to achieve. This can be difficult. There are often nuances and details of the task in hand that must be explicitly identified because they are important to the teacher's idea of what it means to fulfil the criteria for success. Showing pupils several pieces of exemplar material can make this job easier by conveying the elements of success.

After pupils are clear about what they are to achieve the teacher has to work with them to identify what they must do to succeed. Sometimes this can be accomplished by allowing the pupils to form a picture of what the finished result will look like; at other times the topic will need breaking down into small steps. This, again, is an important part of the teacher's role despite the pressures of time. However, if pupils are to become highly skilled learners, this role is a vital one for the teacher.

Once the teacher has established what the pupil is to achieve and how the pupil can achieve it, the pupil is in a position to guide their own learning. The pupil can seek help from suitable sources such as books, other learners and the teacher. When they know what they are trying to accomplish they can forge ahead without reference to the teacher if that is appropriate. This frees the teacher to provide help where it is really needed. When pupils take responsibility in this way their performance standards can rise across the board. It is true that some pupils will resist this, wanting to blame the teacher rather than themselves for their lack of learning, but such methods are surprisingly successful if persisted with. One school helping pupils to guide their learning is asking them to complete a diary. At the end of each lesson pupils write a short account of what they have learned during the lesson and what they can now do or what they now understand.

Pupils who are well versed in the skills of self-assessment are able to rely on their own judgement. If they are able to judge their work against the standard set by the teacher, to compare and determine what meets the standard and what is still lacking, they can develop a true sense of their own capability and where they need to go to next. They can become self-reliant learners.

One of the particular problems in a busy classroom is having time to find out about all the pupils' progress and problems. If time is spent on good-quality self-assessment then teachers can have records of what each of their pupils has been able to do and what they need to do next. This record needs to be carefully thought out to meet the needs of the pupils and teachers, and to allow a dialogue between the two. It can be a valuable way to allow teachers to keep track of all pupils.

Section 2: Using effective questioning techniques

This section is about using oral questioning as a tool for *assessment for learning*. It can help teachers to reflect on how they can:

- use questions to find out what pupils know, understand and can do;
- analyse pupils' responses and their questions in order to find out what they know, understand and can do;
- use questions to find out what pupils' specific misconceptions are in order to target teaching more effectively;
- use pupils' questions to assess understanding.

Using questions effectively

Some questions are better than others at providing teachers with assessment opportunities. Changing the way a question is phrased can make a significant difference to:

- the thought processes pupils need to go through;
- the language demands made on pupils;
- the extent to which pupils reveal their understanding;
- the number of questions needed to make an assessment of pupils' current understanding.

For example, a teacher wants to find out if pupils know the properties of prime numbers:

> The teacher asks **Is 7 a prime number?**

> A pupil responds, **Err. . .Yes, I think so**, or **No, it's not.**

This question has not enabled the teacher to make an effective assessment of whether the pupil knows the properties of prime numbers. Changing the question to **Why is 7 an example of a prime number?** does several things.

1. It helps pupils recall their knowledge of the properties of prime numbers and the properties of 7 and compare them. They then decide whether 7 is an example of a prime number.
2. It requires pupils to explain their understanding of prime numbers and use this to justify their reasoning.
3. The response requires a higher degree of articulation than, **Err.... Yes, I think so.** An answer to the question might be: **Yes, because prime numbers have exactly two factors and 7 has exactly two factors. So 7 is a prime number.**
4. It provides an opportunity to make an assessment without necessarily asking supplementary questions. The question, **Is 7 a prime number?** requires follow-up questions to get a full response on which to make an assessment.

The question **Why is 7 an example of a prime number?** is an example of the general question **Why is *x* an example of *y*?** This is one type of question that is effective in providing assessment opportunities.

Examples of effective questioning techniques

Here are some other types of questions that are also effective in providing assessment opportunities:

- How can we be sure that...?
- What is the same and what is different about...?
- Is it ever/always true/false that...?
- Why do _, _, _ all give the same answer?
- How do you...?
- How would you explain...?
- What does that tell us about...?
- What is wrong with...?
- Why is _ true?

Examples

Topic	Effective assessment questions	Less effective assessment questions
Calculations	What is the same and what is different about addition and subtraction?	3 + - = 7 7 - 3 = -
	Why do 17 + 9, 18 + 8 and 19 + 7 all give the same answer?	What is 17 + 9, 18 + 8 and 19 + 7?
	Why do 6 + 7 and 7 + 6 give the same answer?	What is 6 + 7 and 7 + 6?
	How do you add 9?	What is 7 + 9?
	What is wrong with this calculation? (178 + 167 = 615) [see page 13, illustration 4.1]	What is 178 + 167?
	Why is it true that 4 + 4 + 4 is the same as 3 x 4?	What is 4 + 4 + 4?
Properties of shapes	Why is this picture an example of a shape that has symmetry?	Where are the lines of symmetry on these pictures?
	How do you explain why the angles in any quadrilateral add up to 360°?	What do the angles in this quadrilateral add up to?
	Explain the way you have sorted these shapes.	What shapes have you put in this group?

Properties of triangles	How do we know that these triangles are congruent?	Are these triangles congruent?
	How do we know that this is a triangle?	What shape is this?
Fractions and decimals	What is the same and what is different about decimals and fractions?	What is $1/3$ as a decimal?
Calculating fractions of quantities	How do you find $2/3$ of a number?	What is $2/3$ of 24?
Number operations	Is it always true that multiplying makes numbers bigger?	What is 17 × 0.3?
	Is it always true that when we halve a number the answer is a whole number?	What is half of 5?
Functions and graphs	What does this tell us about graphs of linear equations? (Looking at the graphs of 6 linear equations plotted on the same axes.)	What is the graph of $y = 2x + 5$ going to look like? (Looking at the graph of $y = 2x + 4$.)
Numbers and the number system	What does that tell us about multiples of 5?	Is 36 a multiple of 5?
Probability	Why is selecting a red card from a normal pack an example of an event that has an even chance?	What is the chance of selecting a red card from a normal pack?
Processing data	What is wrong with saying, 'The average shoe size of our class is 5.7?'	What is the average shoe size of our class?
Number properties	Why is the statement, 'an odd number plus an odd number equals an even number' true?	What is an odd number plus an odd number?

Analysing pupils' responses to questions

Asking effective assessment questions is one part of the process of using questions for assessment. Listening carefully to pupils' responses and interpreting them are the other two essential parts of the process. Interpreting the pupil's response is the key to making an assessment about the pupil's current level of understanding and misconceptions.

Here are some responses and assessment notes triggered by the question,
Why is 7 an example of a prime number?

Response	Assessment notes
I dunno.	The pupil might not know what the definition of a prime number is. Alternatively, the pupil may not know that the question involves factors or they might know that the question involves factors but not be able to factorise 7. A supplementary question is required to assess the specific nature of the difficulty.
Because it's odd.	The pupil has a misconception that odd numbers are prime numbers.
Nothing goes into it.	The pupil knows the question is asking them about factors but they haven't recognised that 1 and 7 are factors of 7.
Because it'll only divide by 1 and 7.	The pupil understands the concept of prime numbers and knows that 7 is a prime number. However, they haven't used the correct vocabulary and they haven't verbalised a generalisation about the properties of prime numbers.
Because it's only got two factors; itself and one. Prime numbers only have two.	The pupil has a generalised concept about the properties of prime numbers, understands that 7 is a prime number and can use the correct vocabulary to describe their understanding.

Here are some responses and assessment notes triggered by the question,
How can we be sure that this is a triangle? after showing the class a plastic scalene triangle not in horizontal orientation.

Response	Assessment notes
Don't know.	The pupil may not know the properties of triangles and/or may not be able to identify the properties of the particular shape being held up.
It's red.	The pupil has made an incorrect generalisation about the properties of triangles, possibly through only working with red triangles.
It's got slanty sides.	The pupil understands that one property of triangles is related to sides and their orientation towards each other but has not understood the other properties of triangles.
There's three points.	The pupil understands that one property of triangles is related to the number of vertices but has not understood the other properties of triangles.
It's got three straight sides and three corners.	The pupil has a generalised concept about the properties of triangles and is able to identify specific cases. The pupil may not know the word 'vertices'.

Here are some responses and assessment notes triggered by the question,
Why is the statement 'an odd number plus an odd number equals an even number' true?

Response	Assessment notes
I don't know.	The pupil may not know the properties of odd and/or even numbers. The pupil may not be able to develop a line of mathematical reasoning in order to be convincing about a generalisation.
2 and 2 is 4.	The pupil doesn't know the properties of odd and even numbers. Additionally, the pupil thinks that giving a specific example is sufficient to justify a generalisation.
Because 3 and 5 make 8.	The pupil has given a specific example that shows they understand the properties of odd and even numbers. However the pupil thinks that giving a specific example is sufficient to justify a generalisation.
Because they pair up.	The pupil understands the properties of odd and even numbers, and has begun to develop an appropriate line of reasoning to support the generalisation. However, the pupil thinks that giving a specific example is sufficient to justify a generalisation and hasn't sufficiently developed communication skills.
Because every odd number has an extra bit, so if you put them together that makes another pair and even numbers are about pairs.	The pupil understands the properties of odd and even numbers, and has developed an appropriate line of reasoning to explain the generalisation and describe this clearly. The pupil has not yet begun to express this symbolically.

Using questions to find out pupils' specific misconceptions

Sometimes a pupil's response to an initial question does not provide enough information to make an assessment. It may then be necessary to follow up with further questions, engaging in a dialogue with the pupil. This allows a fuller assessment of the pupil's understanding.

In this example the teacher is able to make assessments about the pupil's understanding of a standard written algorithm for addition. During the dialogue the teacher asks questions to clarify his or her initial assessments.

	Dialogue	Assessment notes
T	The pupil who did this calculation made a mistake. Can you find out what it is? [See illustration 4.1 below]	
P	I can't see anything wrong with it.	May not be secure in understanding of place value in written algorithms, or able to estimate. Not immediately able to follow someone else's line of reasoning.
T	How could YOU check it?	
P	Well, 178 is about 200 and so is 167 and that makes about 400, so the answer is too big.	Able to round to the nearest 100 and estimate appropriately.
T	How can you work out where this person has gone wrong?	
P	I'll do it myself. [see illustration 4.2 below] The answer is 345. Their answer's too big.	Can use an informal written method, adding the most significant digit first. Shows an understanding of place value.
T	So what mistake did this pupil make?	
P	They got too many hundreds.	Pupil able to compare two numbers and able to spot the most significant error in the calculation.
T	How did that happen?	
P	They've got these little numbers, but I don't know where they've come from.	Pupil not familiar with this standard written method.

Illustration 4.1

$$
\begin{array}{r}
178 \\
+\ 167 \\
{}_{4\ \ 1} \\
\hline
615
\end{array}
$$

Illustration 4.2

$$
\begin{array}{r}
178 \\
+\ 167 \\
\hline
200 \\
130 \\
15 \\
\hline
345
\end{array}
$$

Final assessment:

- pupil understands place value in three-digit numbers;
- pupil able to round three-digit numbers to the nearest 100;
- pupil able to estimate the answers to calculations;
- pupil able to use an informal written method for addition accurately;
- pupil able to identify the most significant error in the result of a calculation;
- pupil not familiar with a standard written method.

Using pupils' questions to assess understanding

Sometimes pupils provide assessment opportunities through the questions they ask. These can provide rich insights into pupils' understandings and misconceptions. The following are a few examples of the things pupils ask and the assessments their teachers make.

Context	Pupil's question	Assessment notes
Fourteen pairs of pupils mark the same three sets of test scripts using their own mark schemes. Results are then compared.	Sir, could we tell how good our mark schemes are by using distance from the mean?	Pupil has a good grasp of mean and range and is ready to learn about standard deviation.
Pupils use calculators to perform calculations involving more than one operation.	Miss, me and my friend have got different answers, which one is right? (Pointing to the calculator screen after performing the calculation $3 + 4 \times 2$.)	Pupil doesn't understand conventions about order of operations and the way different calculators handle this.
Discussing likely and unlikely events.	My dad says that he's bound to win the lottery one day because he buys two tickets every week. That's right isn't it?	Pupil doesn't understand that lottery draws are independent events.
Classification of quadrilaterals.	Is a square a rectangle, miss?	Pupil has generalised the properties of a rectangle and is testing out whether a square fits this generalisation.
Pupils working on the addition of fractions.	Please sir, is this right? ($\frac{1}{3} + \frac{1}{4} = \frac{2}{7}$)	Pupils don't understand what the numerators and denominators represent in fraction notation.

Section 3: Using marking and feedback strategies

Many reports suggest that pupils at all levels of attainment do not make learning gains when work is graded or given 'marks out of 10'. Gains come from comments that tell pupils what they have demonstrated about their learning to the teacher, and what they need to do next to improve.

When marking pupils' work, teachers need to make a clear distinction between assessment *of* learning and assessment *for* learning. Effective assessment for learning with constructive, objective comments can help to raise standards.

It is common practice for teachers to return marked mathematics work to pupils. This may include ticks and crosses that correspond to the score out of a possible maximum. Teachers' intentions in giving the number of right and wrong items are partly so that pupils can make a judgement about how effectively they have performed against the learning objectives. There may also be stars, smiley faces, team points and written or spoken comments. Reasons for giving rewards such as stars include reinforcing appropriate responses, expressing approval and celebrating success. Comments, which may be written or spoken, serve a variety of purposes, which may or may not relate to the main learning objective. For instance, teachers may comment on pupils' presentation of, or perceived attitude to, the work with comments like **One digit per square**, or **Careless**.

Research has shown that pupils who are given only written or spoken comments on how they can improve their work and are not given marks or grades make greater learning gains than pupils given marks or grades only. Those given a combination of both marks and comments, which is possibly the most widely used form of feedback in our education system, make less progress than those given only comments.

A study by Ruth Butler (1988) in Israeli schools analysed pupils' work marked by one of the following strategies:

- comments and actions for improvement;
- grades only;
- praise only;
- no feedback at all.

The quality of work of those given only comments and actions for improvement improved substantially from lesson to lesson. Those given praise only, or grades only, did no better than the pupils who were given no feedback at all.

Rewards for learning

Similarly, there is evidence to support the importance of considering how attitudes to learning can be affected by a classroom culture focused on extrinsic awards. The practice is based on the idea that pupils will strive harder to learn in order to gain rewards. But we need to consider the effect on pupils who, despite their best efforts, do not score highly enough to receive a token. Educators warn about the risks that accompany this:

> The traditional way of encouraging children to want to learn the things that we want to teach is by giving rewards for success: prizes privileges, gold stars. Two grave risks attend this practice. The first is obvious to common sense, the second much less so.
>
> The obvious risk is to the children who do not get the stars, for this is just one way of defining them as failures. The other risk is to all of the children – 'winners' and 'losers' alike. There is now a substantial amount of evidence pointing to the conclusion that if an activity is rewarded by some extrinsic prize or token – something quite external to the activity itself – then that activity is less likely to be engaged in later in a free and voluntary manner when the rewards are absent, and it is less likely to be enjoyed.
>
> *Children's Minds* (Donaldson, M, 1990, p 115)

In addition to these 'grave risks', giving rewards such as stars and team points, and comparing pupils with one another can have other negative effects on learning. Those who get low scores and fewer token rewards come to believe they lack ability and therefore cannot improve. The less obvious negative impact is on the higher attainers. They may look for ways to get the best marks and the most rewards, rather than ways to improve their learning.

In considering the negative effects of extrinsic awards, we need to consider pupils' motivation and self-esteem. A culture of success should be promoted where every pupil can make achievements by building on their previous performance, rather than being compared with others. This is based on informing pupils about the strengths and weaknesses demonstrated in their work, and giving feedback about what their next steps should be.

Purposes of marking and feedback

The purpose of returning marked work to pupils or of oral feedback is to enable pupils to improve their learning. However, both teachers and pupils need to be clear about the assessment criteria that will inform marking and feedback. For instance, if the learning objectives for the work to be marked were not concerned with presentation and neatness, teachers may consider whether comments about those things should be made, particularly if it is the only comment that is made. In order for feedback to be effective, pupils need to be aware of the assessment criteria. In *Teacher assessment in core subjects at key stage 2* (Ofsted, 1998), 75 schools were selected where there was relatively good practice, but even here pupils were seldom aware of teachers' assessment objectives.

Teachers also need to decide whether the results of marking should always be shared with pupils. For example, they might decide not to give feedback about work if it was set solely to inform them about pupil groupings. When teachers feed back to pupils about their progress, this will be effective when pupils are aware of what they are meant to be learning and how this can be achieved.

> Where anyone is trying to learn, feedback about their efforts has three elements – *the desired goal*, the evidence about their *present position*, and some understanding of *a way to close the gap* between the two.
>
> [Sadler, 1989]

This assumes that pupils need to be actively involved in their own learning, for example through assessing their own work. Evidence from inspections shows that assessment to help pupils learn is one of the weakest aspects of teaching practice. Assessment usually excludes the pupil or, where it does involve the pupil, is often only to save teachers' time.

How can marking and feedback be improved?

In marking pupils' work, teachers can consider:

- how well the pupil has understood the task;
- what the pupil knows and does not know;
- what the pupil needs to do next to improve;
- how the pupil will be informed of this;
- how they can encourage pupils to review their work critically and constructively.

Teachers who use a range of effective techniques for assessment, marking and feedback are more likely to be successful in raising standards.

Feedback from pupils about teachers' marking and feedback

In order to improve practice, it is important to find out what pupils think about the purposes of marking, how it is done and who does it. The following comments were made by 12 infant and junior children on what they like or dislike about having work marked, and why they think it is done. Every year group except year 5 was represented. When asked the most important reason for marking, half the comments referred to scores (the number of correct and incorrect items) and half to helping children to improve their work.

How do children feel about marking?

- All the children liked having their work marked.
- Fourteen out of 21 comments made in response to this question expressed a liking for ticks and encouragement, particularly the younger children.
- All the children disliked crosses.
- Two children preferred comments to ticks.

- One child expressed concern about lack of explanation in marking.
- Half of the children said they preferred writing or talking to be part of marking:

> Talking is best because it doesn't make a mess of your work.

> They [comments] tell you what to do.

> They [comments] help you remember.

From children's participation in this survey, it would seem that they like having work marked and are willing to act upon what the teachers say. It is therefore important that we say the right things to them to support and help them take their next steps in learning.

Why and how do teachers mark work?

- Fifty-eight per cent of responses focused on whether the work was 'right or wrong'.
- From year 2 onwards a wider view on marking was developing: **It helps you see it in your mind.**
- Year 6 children's comments focused on how marking can help you improve.
- Ticks, crosses, **good** and **well done** were all familiar to children. These were associated with the number of correct and incorrect answers.
- Children said that comments help them improve. These generally referred to presentation and rate of work.
- Children said that the frequently used comment **See me** made them think **What have I done wrong?** They also felt this comment was positive because then they would know **what to do.**
- Marking that asked questions was, in their experience, limited.

Who do children think should mark their work?

Children were asked to consider the possibility of other children, themselves, other adults (for example classroom assistants) and parents marking their work.

- All children thought only teachers should mark their work.
- Children were concerned that, unlike teachers, other adults were not experts.
- Linked to the above, children felt it was good that parents might be involved, but concerned that they would **get it wrong.**
- Marking other children's work was considered to be **fun,** with no other serious purpose.
- In terms of marking their own work, they again referred to **fun** but two children raised the point that it was an opportunity for self-assessment.

What do children do as a result of marking?

- Of the 12 children, nine said they had to do corrections.
- Children may have to talk to the teacher, for example if the teacher has written **See me.**

Children discussing the results of calculations

A group of six year 5 children were given the following calculations:

- $363 \div 3 =$
- $6000 \div 6 =$
- $34 \div 7 =$
- $6 \div 12 =$
- $68 \div 17 =$
- $4 \div \frac{1}{2} =$
- How many 30g servings can you get from a 500g packet of cereal?

The children worked on these calculations on their own. When they had all finished, they compared each answer in turn and discussed it.

$363 \div 3$

They all had the same (correct) answer for this example, but could give various different written or mental methods that all arrived at the same solution. They concluded that it must be correct.

$6000 \div 6$

Again, they all got the same answer and could explain to each other how they had arrived at it.

$34 \div 7$

They had various different solutions for this one:

- 7 r 6
- 28 r 4 (2 children)
- 5
- 28 r 6 (2 children)

They knew that it was necessary to come to an agreement about what was the correct answer, so used a calculator. They concluded that the answer was 4 and **some gobbledygook** (4.8571428).

One of the children (answer 28 r 6) then realised that in searching for the multiple of 7 before 35 (28) she had focused on the multiple. She announced her moment of insight by saying, **Ah, I see what I've done.** She explained that her answer was incorrect because it would mean that there were 28 sevens in 34 with a remainder of 6. She realised that she should be focusing on the number of groups of 7 in 28. She concluded that the answer was 4 r 6 and by this time everyone else who had 28 as the main part of the answer agreed, and could also see that they had made a simple error in calculating the remainder.

They could all explain their answers:

- the child whose answer was 5 felt that as 7 x 5 = 35, an answer of 5 was near enough;
- the child whose answer was 7 r 6 was able to say that he had forgotten which of the factors, 7 or 4, he needed after calculating the remainder.

6 ÷ 12

Five children thought the answer was 2 and one, negative 6. The first five had all interpreted it was 12 divided by 6. The other child knew that this was incorrect, but admitted that he doubted his own answer (-6). The others, though, thought that it had potential. They discussed whether division was commutative and finally agreed that it was not. Once again a calculator was used. They were happy with the solution of 0.5 and translated it into one-half. They still felt that the negative number idea was good and fitted in with the idea that division was not commutative. They were not sure that 0.5 was right.

68 ÷ 17

Two children had correct solutions of 4, two had 55, one had 5 and one had no answer.

The two successful children had found the solution by doubling 17 to get 34 (2 x 17), then doubling 34 to get 68 (4 x 17). The others agreed that 4 was the correct answer. Both children who had 55 said that they had added 17 + 17 + 17 and got 55. They then realised that another 17 would be more than 68. They realised that they had focused on the 'multiple' again. The child who had 5 had made a guess and the child who had not attempted it said she was leaving it until last because it looked more complex than some of the others.

4 ÷ ½

All of the children, apart from one who had decided not to attempt it, had the correct solution of 8. They said they had interpreted the question as **How many halves in 4?**

How many 30g servings can you get from a 500g packet of cereal?

No one had attempted the word problem but, as they discussed the fact that all word problems are difficult, one of them suddenly said, **Four servings would be 120g.** The children then jointly proceeded to 'double up' until they got to 480g and 16 servings, and 20g.

The whole session lasted from 9.10am until 9.30am. The children agreed that discussing work with other children gave them an insight into their own errors and an opportunity to explore alternative methods of calculation. They also felt that teacher intervention may be necessary in some cases.

Getting children to self-correct

When children have been working, they could be encouraged to look over their work to check whether there are any obvious errors. This gives them an opportunity to use techniques such as checking answers by using inverse operations, using an equivalent calculation or doing the calculation in a different order and using their knowledge of odd and even numbers. Putting the responsibility for this kind of marking onto the child should also help them to become more diligent about making approximations using rounding before they do calculations.

This is what happened when some year 3 and 4 children were involved in marking their own work.

The learning objective was to teach children a written method of subtraction. This involved two-digit numbers and the method of partitioning and decomposition. Typical examples of problems were:

- 49 – 15 =
- 56 – 17 =
- 41 – 29 =

The reason for using numbers that children should be able to calculate mentally was so that they would be able to use a mental method to check their answers and so gain trust in the written method. Examples were presented 'horizontally' as shown. Some of the children used the following methods.

Method 1 – for example, to calculate 56 – 17

(Partition into tens and units and set out 'vertically')

$$
\begin{array}{r}
50 + 6 \\
- \ 10 + 7 \\
\hline
\end{array}
$$

Next step:

(Subtract 10 from the 50 leaving 40 and add the 10 to the 6 making the 6 up to 16, effectively partitioning 56 into 40 and 16)

$$
\begin{array}{r}
40 + 16 \\
- \ 10 + 7 \\
\hline
30 + 9 \\
\end{array}
$$

(Answer: 39)

Method 2 – for example, to calculate 49 – 15

Some children in the same class recorded a different method:

(Subtract the tens) $40 - 10 = 30$

(Subtract the units) $9 - 5 = 4$

(Add the partial results) $30 + 4 = 34$

(Answer: 34)

NB Many children find this method confusing as the result of the second subtraction may be a negative number.

After they had attempted several examples, teachers looked at the work and noted any errors. The work was not marked with ticks or crosses.

Children were then told that on a particular page there was an error and asked if they could find it themselves. When they had found it, they were to explain to a teacher where the error lay and give the correct answer.

The children who had understood and could explain the method, and who were confident about checking with a mental method, could analyse and correct the errors that they had made. However, in every case they did not find it easy to pick out the examples with errors – these had to be pointed out.

Spotting errors

The type of errors that these children made tended to be simple errors in calculation. For example, in 56 – 17:

$$40 + 16$$
$$\underline{10 + 7}$$
$$30 + 11 = 41 \text{ (answer)}$$

When this example was pointed out the child said: **16 take away 7 is not 11, it's 9: the answer is 39.**

Several children could not analyse the errors they had made, even when they were pointed out. This applied to children using both methods. As well as being unable to spot their errors, these children were unable to explain the method they were using.

The children who did understand the method were able to check each example by simply going through the procedure and checking that all the calculations were correct. The children who did not understand the method had no way of checking if what they were doing was correct because they were following a procedure that did not make complete sense to them.

For example, in 89 – 65:

$$80 - 60 = 10$$
$$9 - 5 = 4$$
$$10 + 4 = 14 \text{ (answer)}$$

The child could not find the error, only explain the steps in the procedure. Children in this category seemed locked into following the procedure. The principle seemed to be that if you follow the rules in the right order you will get the right answer; they were therefore unable to look at only part of the procedure. The child in this example was unable to find the error, even when the exact (incorrect) calculation was pointed out.

There was another category of children. For example, to calculate 41 − 29 the child had written:

$$
\begin{array}{r}
\overset{30}{\cancel{40}} + 11 \\
20 + 9 \\
\hline
30 + 11
\end{array}
$$

(Answer: 41)

Her explanation:

> write 40 + 1;
> write 20 + 9 underneath;
> cross out 40 and put 10 onto 1;
> add 30 and 11 (41);

She did not realise that in seeking a solution she had arrived back at the original problem. When asked if she had an alternative method, she explained:

> 40 take away 20 (20);
> 1 take away 9 (8). She was told this was incorrect;
> Oh! It will go into negative numbers – it's minus 8;
> so 20 minus 8 is 12;
> the answer is 12.

All the children who understood the task could correct their own errors. Those who did not understood the task demonstrated this by being unable to self-correct.

This raises the issues:

- is it necessary to mark every calculation if the children can find their own errors, and the errors are few in number?;
- children who cannot self-correct may well not understand what has been taught.

Schools in focus: Sharing their practice

Four case studies were undertaken in the following schools:

1 Blenheim Infants School

2 Bolton Brow Junior and Infant School

3 The Blake School (secondary)

4 Churchill Community School (comprehensive)

The case studies are focused on developments in their schools covering the period 1998-2000.

Case study 1:
Blenheim Infants School

Background

Blenheim Infants School is a two-form entry infant school in the south of the London borough of Bromley. Although Bromley is predominantly a leafy middle-class area, the north and south of the borough does have areas of social deprivation and poverty. To one side of the school is a large housing association estate consisting mainly of low- and high-rise flats. The unemployed white working-class largely represents the area although there are a small number of black and Asian families, travellers and refugees. There is a high proportion of single parent families and a number of 'problem families' have been re-housed on the estate from other parts of the borough.

To the other side of the school is an estate of middle-class 1930s houses. This side of Bromley is relatively well served with primary schools, some of which have prestigious reputations, but recent building and increasing popularity has meant these schools are very difficult to get into. Blenheim has, as a result, tended to take most of the children from the estate as well as children who have either not been able to get into the school of their choice or whose parents live locally and want their children to attend a school with a 'mixed' intake.

Historically at Blenheim there has always been a high number of children receiving free school meals and with social or emotional problems. Children often come into school with low baseline assessment scores and poor language and social skills. As a result, some have problems adopting acceptable behaviour for a school environment.

This case study illustrates how self-assessment and sharing clear learning objectives (target-setting) with children can be used.

The learning environment

Establishing effective learning

Over the last five years the ethos at the school has changed slowly and gradually, yet quite dramatically. Many parents are unemployed; they are often lacking in key education skills and tend to have very low self-esteem. While they want the best for their children, their own experiences sometimes mean that they have very low expectations. This then has a negative impact on their children. The behaviour of a small but significant minority of children was at times appalling. Parents did not always value school and education generally and, as a result, relationships between school and parents were not always as helpful as they could be. The teaching staff were spending too much time and energy on discipline to the detriment of the children's learning.

To improve the situation and to give staff and children a forum to express and discuss their feelings, 'circle time' was introduced as a regular feature of school life. This soon became one of the children's favourite times of the week and began to make a real difference to the school ethos as the children realised that their opinions were valued.

Another forward step was made by introducing a very carefully thought out positive discipline policy in the infant and partner junior schools. With clear and simple class rules, consistent and fair graded sanctions for misbehaviour, and a very desirable set of incentives for good behaviour, behaviour at the school improved rapidly and dramatically. The children responded to such an extent that a further 'good citizen' scheme was introduced which included parents and the local community. It helped to make parents feel more involved in the school community and to raise the profile of the school in the local area.

Self-assessment

Rationale for self-evaluation and target-setting

'Circle time' and the positive discipline policy improved behaviour and raised the children's self-esteem, but they still appeared to be unaware that they should be part of their own learning process. The assessment coordinator hoped that involving the children in a self-evaluation, target-setting and appraisal process would help the children to appreciate that they were responsible for, and could be in control of, their own learning and that this could in turn improve their results.

The school tried out the self-evaluation aspect of the process with the year 2 children. As an introduction, the assessment coordinator and the other year 2 class teacher spent time building on the values already established, emphasising the importance of valuing each other's points of view and contribution. Efforts were made to develop the learning environment so that the children felt even safer to take risks, make mistakes, ask questions and share misconceptions. The children were constantly reminded that they were responsible for ensuring that they understood.

Establishing and evaluating the qualities needed to be a learner

The next step was to establish with the children the qualities they felt were necessary to effective learning. Early in the summer term of 1998, the assessment coordinator used self-evaluation sheets designed for key stages 2 and 3 as a guide. During a whole-class discussion she encouraged the children to produce a list of qualities appropriate to their age.

This sheet was then made into a 'user-friendly' self-evaluation sheet that the children completed on their own after an introduction reminding them how important it was to be honest. The children then sat with a 'friendly partner' and moderated each other's sheets. They were reminded to make helpful comments to their partner and to always consider each other's feelings. The children were then asked to choose one of the qualities where they had recorded that they had not been very successful or, if none, a quality where they had assessed themselves 'OK'. They wrote at the bottom of the sheets where they would like to improve.

The teachers sorted the sheets into similar areas of weakness. It was fascinating to note that, in practically all cases, the children had recognised the same area for improvement as the teacher herself had identified. The few exceptions were among the more immature children and those with special educational needs. These children did not understand what they were expected to do or were incapable of judging their own strengths and weaknesses. Interestingly, practically all children with behavioural problems correctly identified their own areas of weakness.

Monitoring progress

Each child was provided with a card folder containing an individualised target-monitoring sheet to be completed at the end of each day for a week. The children judged how far they had met their targets that day by colouring in the appropriate positions. At the end of the week it was easy for the children to see whether they were making progress towards meeting their targets. The teacher was also able to monitor the progress of individual children and pick up on any that were not making progress, the idea being that, if the targets were realistic and achievable, children should achieve them and be able to move on to other targets within six weeks. If the targets were not met then they needed to be renegotiated and reset.

The children enjoyed monitoring their own progress and were brutally honest about their performance. Children could, on the whole, understand the criteria for success and were then able to use this to assess their own performance and to recognise whether they had made an obvious improvement. In addition, the teacher or their peers gave verbal praise and feedback, measuring progress in activities such as reading books, spelling ladders and number challenges. For behavioural targets, the child was able to measure success by the number of 'bonus points' and 'merit awards' earned, and, conversely, failure to fully meet a behavioural target by the number of 'time-outs', 'isolations' and 'golden times' lost.

Extending self-evaluation

Due to the success of the self-evaluation sheets with year 2 children it was decided to extend the process into year 1 so that the children were prepared for self-evaluation and target-setting when they arrived in year 2.
The two year 1 teachers went through a similar self-evaluation process with the children. This also took place in the summer term and teachers had release time for interviewing children.

The year 1 teachers considered the process to be successful with some adaptations. For example, the children needed a lot of support to complete the self-evaluation sheets, particularly with the reading. Some children were too immature to evaluate themselves properly and those with behavioural problems often failed to recognise that they had any problems at all. The school decided to dispense with the 'friendly partner' to moderate sheets for year 1 children and instead the teacher moderated at the individual interview.

Here, teacher and child discussed the sheet and the child's progress in general and set targets together. These targets were more teacher-led and tended to be either behavioural or general learning targets, but were generally similar to those set for year 2 children. The targets were then shared with parents at an open evening and passed on to the year 2 teacher in the September. This self-evaluation process was repeated with year 1 in the 1999 summer term in readiness for a full year of self-evaluation and target-setting in year 2.

Developing self-evaluation, target-setting and self-appraisal

In late autumn 1998, the new year 2 children were introduced to a fuller self-evaluation, target-setting and appraisal process. As with the previous year, the two teachers spent time establishing the right atmosphere and values in the class. When the time was right the children completed a self-evaluation sheet, had their sheet moderated by a 'friendly partner' and were interviewed by the teacher. These year 2 children had already been through the simplified process in July as year 1 children and took to the ideas much more quickly than the previous year 2 group. At the interview, the two sheets were compared and the teachers made a point of helping each child to identify progress made during the intervening period as well as pinpointing an area for improvement.

Target-setting

At this stage some children's targets were still either behavioural or attitudinal, but the majority were more work related. The most popular being:

- getting on and concentrating;
- finishing tasks/working faster;
- not giving up;
- asking if don't understand;
- checking work properly;
- neater handwriting;
- neater presentation;
- better spelling;
- better reading;
- better mathematics.

Two days' supply cover was arranged to enable both class teachers to spend time with each child individually so that they could discuss the child's progress and make new targets together. Every child was interviewed for 10 to 15 minutes. At each interview teacher and child discussed the self-evaluation sheet and the child's reasons for his or her judgements. At the end of the interview the teacher and child agreed on one or two targets for the child, usually based on areas for improvement.

Children and teachers thoroughly enjoyed this precious opportunity to talk to each other at length on a one-to-one basis. In general, the children's views of themselves were very honest and incredibly perceptive. The experience certainly had an impact on classroom practice and highlighted just how much schools can underestimate the capabilities of young children.

At the next parents' meeting, the teachers' and children's targets were shared so that parents, teacher and child were all involved in the process. It is a salutary thought that, in the past, teachers have discussed progress and targets with parents but have not thought to share this information with the child concerned.

Using prompts

Many children expressed the feeling that they knew they should do certain things but had problems remembering to do so. After discussion, a system of personalised prompts was devised to help the children remember their target. The children suggested their own slogans to act as a reminder, and some of these were:

- Get a move on!
- Think about the sound, think about the look!
- Speed up, join up!
- I can do it!
- Check your work!

The slogans were word processed boldly and mounted on to a colourful card, which could then be displayed on each child's desk. These proved to be very popular and did remind the children of their targets.

Improvements strategies

Specific strategies for improving children's work in the literacy hour and daily mathematics lesson

Many children expressed the wish to be 'better' at mathematics. Again, the teacher used her expertise and knowledge of the child to identify a specific skill or area that the child, or a group of children with similar targets, could work on. These included refining, checking and estimating techniques, and also specific aspects of mathematics such as knowledge of number bonds, doubles and halves, odds and evens, and understanding place value. The literacy hour and daily mathematics lesson actually made building in time for teaching and practising these skills and concepts easier. Particular strategies were introduced into the classroom to improve techniques for checking work and developing mental mathematics skills. These strategies are described below.

Checking work

It was always the case that when the children finished any written work they would bring it straight to the teacher. She would glance at it, immediately see errors of spelling or punctuation that the child need not have made and send them back to their desk, asking them to **check their work**. From the individual interviews it soon became apparent that many children wanted to get better at **checking their work** but had no idea how to do so.

To meet this need, graded checklists were introduced according to the ability of the literacy group. The children could refer to these checklists to help them inspect their work and make any necessary alterations. As a result, written work improved quickly and dramatically. This had an additional effect of helping children meet other targets relating to spelling, punctuation and vocabulary choices.

Developing mental mathematics skills

To improve children's mental calculation strategies and mental recall, the two teachers introduced a daily mathematics challenge to take place for five to 10 minutes every day at the beginning of the mathematics lesson. This challenge gave children an opportunity to rehearse and develop skills such as recalling number bonds to 10. This followed on from work on the different ways of making 10 with two numbers, how to calculate by counting on or back, and odd and even number, patterns involved, etc. All children were provided with a set of number cards to take home and practise with, first calculating and then learning.

After a few days, children were given the opportunity to demonstrate their ability either to calculate or recall the bonds. The teachers first explained to the class the concept of monitoring personal improvement and beating your own record rather than someone else's. As the atmosphere in the classroom was now one of mutual support and celebration for individual progress, this was not a problem and the children soon grew accustomed to applauding everyone who 'had a go', regardless of their actual score.

There were some surprises. Children who had previously not been prepared to be singled out were often willing to try this, and those children commonly regarded as 'clever' by their peers were not necessarily the best at the challenges.

Over the term the challenges changed depending on the class's needs and the mathematics focus. Further challenges involved using knowledge of number bonds to 10 to calculate other numbers, doubles, halves and multiplying by 5 or 10.

As 'public records' were kept of each child's performance, it was easy for children to monitor their own progress. The number challenge was entirely voluntary. Some children waited and practised for a long time before 'accepting the challenge' and having a go. A few children never volunteered but, despite this, they showed an improvement in these areas. This was probably because the children watching were expected to do the same challenge in their heads during each number challenge session. Also, after each challenge it became common practice to discuss the different methods each child used.

Measuring the project's success

It is very difficult to actually measure the success of a project of this nature as there were so many different outcomes, the majority of which are qualitative and so cannot be measured. However, the overriding impression was that the project was a real success and worth continuing, despite some limitations.

Limitations

The whole process initially took a long time to set up and, even when established, time had to be allocated within the class for monitoring and resetting targets. The teachers also needed to allow time at the end of each day for the children to complete their monitoring sheets. Some children found self-evaluation difficult and needed more support than others. Also, in year 1 interviews, the target-setting was more teacher-led. Despite this, the majority of the children coped well. Above all, although time is at a premium in the timetable, it was considered that subsequent benefits made spending time on this project worthwhile.

The success of the project depended on release time for teachers to conduct personal interviews. However, since the introduction of the literacy and numeracy strategies, the children are far more used to working independently. It might therefore be possible in the future to conduct interviews in the classroom while the other children are involved in their work, particularly when the children grow accustomed to the self-evaluation and target-setting process.

Outcomes

Improved attitudes

This was felt to be the greatest success. The year 2 children's attitudes improved greatly. They seemed to grow in self-confidence and self-esteem, and also to have more respect for each other. Less time was wasted settling the class down and asking them to concentrate as they were more aware of the reasons for doing so. Attitudes to work and behaviour also continued to improve as the children became more self-disciplined.

Improved performance

As the target-setting and self-appraisal process continued, the children became active partners in their own learning and standards of work improved. This was particularly so in writing and numeracy over this period. Although it is difficult to prove, the school feels that a great deal of this improvement can be attributed to the new ethos in the classroom, the self-evaluation and target-setting process, and the specific numeracy and literacy strategies described in this case study.

End of key stage test results and Ofsted Inspection

Test results in 1998 and 1999 for English and mathematics were above average compared with schools of a similar kind and, in mathematics, above the national average. It is impossible to assess how much of this improvement is due to the project, but the school feels that certainly the 1999 cohort would not have performed as well if it had not been for improvements brought about by the project.

A recent Ofsted inspection 'Main findings' summary highlighted the following points, under 'What the school does well' (Ofsted inspection report on Blenheim Infant School, Bromley, 11 October 1999).

- 'Relationships are very constructive and the pupils are maturing with positive attitudes and good concentration.'

- 'There are excellent systems for teaching about good behaviour and for supporting pupils to achieve what is expected.'

The main body of the report praised aspects of the school's assessment systems and in particular the self-evaluation and target-setting processes:

> Two notable strengths of assessment procedures are pupil self-assessment and target setting, and the prediction at the end of year 1 of levels that pupils might attain in their year 2 National Curriculum tests. The first is effectively focusing pupils on what they need to do and the second is providing useful data for teachers to identify underachievers.

Future

Continuing the process at key stage 1

Due to the success of the project, the school decided to continue with exactly the same process for the year 2 children in autumn 1999. It was still felt that year 1 children were, on the whole, too young to make implementing the full process worthwhile. As revealed in last year's programme, the targets do initially include a number of behavioural, attitudinal and general learning targets. However, as the year progressed and the children met these targets, the new targets became more specific to literacy and mathematics, and it is felt this trend would continue as the children moved on through key stage 2.

Involvement at key stage 2

The assessment coordinator has since approached the neighbouring junior school (situated on the same site but under a different headteacher) to determine whether the school would be prepared to take on the self-evaluation and target-setting process as the year 2 children move into year 3. Discussions are at an initial stage but the school is interested in taking on the scheme, starting with year 3. The self-evaluation and target-setting programme is already in place in some secondary schools in the borough. Consequently, when the self-evaluation process has worked its way through key stage 2, the children will be familiar and comfortable with the process as soon as they start secondary school.

It is appreciated that complete success will depend on other feeder primary schools taking on the self-evaluation and target-setting initiative.

Case study 2: Bolton Brow Junior and Infant School

Background

Bolton Brow Junior and Infant School is situated in the small town of Sowerby Bridge, a suburb of Halifax in West Yorkshire. Sowerby Bridge is a depleted industrial town with considerable unemployment. Most of the children live in small terraced or council housing. They are taught in single-age classes in the main building with a nursery class situated in a separate building. Of the 214 pupils plus the 52 part time in the nursery, 25 per cent are on the special needs register and six have full statements. Attainment on entry to the reception class is below national expectations for this age.

This case study illustrates how the way that a teacher responds to children's work can enhance progress.

The learning environment

At the time of the study, the headteacher had been at the school for three years. He took over in 1996 when the school was performing poorly. A training inspection in 1992 had reported that the management of the curriculum was weak and children's achievement in almost half the lessons was unsatisfactory or poor, including in mathematics. Little progress seemed to have been made and behaviour was very poor between 1992 and 1996. This led to unsettled classrooms and poor learning. The expectation of both children and teachers was low. In 1996 only 21 per cent of children achieved level 4 or above in key stage 2 mathematics national tests and only 33 per cent in English.

Establishing effective learning

As a first step a positive behaviour policy was formulated by all staff and established throughout the school. The curriculum policies and schemes of work were rewritten and expectations of everyone involved with the school were raised.

Within a year a learning environment was established where teachers could teach and children could learn. In 1998 the school received a very favourable Ofsted inspection report. In the main findings, the report stated that: 'The school has succeeded in raising standards across many curricular areas and in improving the level of behaviour throughout the school.' The quality of teaching overall was good; by 1999 nearly 70 per cent of pupils achieved level 4 in mathematics and, in English, 75 per cent.

Development in mathematics

In 1996 the school had no policy or scheme of work for mathematics and many staff did not know what mathematics to teach or how to teach it. The new headteacher was a mathematics specialist and had been the local education authority (LEA) advisory teacher in mathematics. Staff meetings were used to draw up the policy and scheme of work, and used as an opportunity to discuss mathematics teaching. The headteacher, deputy and key stage 1 coordinator monitored progress. Teachers reported that they were now feeling much more confident in teaching mathematics.

The numeracy project

As the headteacher had been involved in the National Numeracy Project, the school decided to implement the scheme in September 1998. Staff meetings were set aside to discuss the project's approach to teaching mathematics and staff took part in a training day on mental work and calculation. They reported that they were enjoying teaching mathematics and felt that the children were more enthusiastic and motivated. Parents were informed about mathematics learning in the weekly newsletter, and the new reception class parents were briefed on how they could help their children at home. Non-teaching assistants (NTAs) were given a short course in the numeracy project, led by the headteacher and they worked daily with the class teacher. As a result, they reported back that they felt more confident in teaching mathematics. Resources were bought and made for each classroom, and materials not used regularly were held centrally.

Feedback strategies

Evaluating the teaching and learning of mathematics

As part of their evaluation of the teaching and learning of mathematics, the staff looked at marking and feedback. They found that children associated ticks and marks on their work with their success or failure in mathematics. Staff agreed that some children had a low opinion of their own mathematical ability because they associated crosses and low marks with failure. However, many children had an understanding of the area of mathematics being taught if their work was looked at and discussed in more detail. Another observation was that children had a poor understanding of how learning took place in mathematics. Many children believed that when they were taught a new mathematical area their learning was poor if they didn't understand it immediately. This would reinforce their perception of failure. To combat this, class teachers were advised to explain regularly to children that learning is a gradual process and they should not always expect to have a full grasp of a concept straight away. Individual children were also to be constantly reminded of their success.

Although attainment in mathematics had vastly improved, some children still lacked confidence and made little or slow progress. It was observed that children as early as key stage 1 were turned off and lacked confidence because they were handed back work with more crosses than ticks. It was also agreed that marking work away from children for the sole purpose of putting ticks and scores on a child's book was time-consuming for the teacher and of little benefit in taking children forward in their learning. With this in mind, the staff put together a short marking policy and guidelines (see pages 36-38). They agreed to use this way of marking for a term and then discuss it further. Teachers, support staff and the headteacher would each monitor evidence of the policy's success.

Self-assessment

Teachers and support staff found out children's thoughts on their work in mathematics by asking them questions and looking at their self-assessment sheets. On the sheets children wrote comments such as: I found ordering and rounding numbers a little bit difficult at first but once we talked about how to do it and had a go I found it easy. A statemented child wrote: the best thing we did was learning how to do division. I found it hard at first but with help I understand it and now I like doing it.

Self-assessment sheets

Staff believed there was immense benefit in children's feedback about how they viewed their learning of mathematics. The school decided that every teacher should set aside time each half-term to talk to children about what they had learned. This was to be mainly done in small groups because of time restraints. It was also agreed that self-assessment sheets would be a beneficial way of children explaining their learning of mathematics. At first the sheets were given to year 6 children at the end of each half-term but staff realised that they could be given out at the start of each half-term and used on an ongoing basis. The self-assessment sheets were based on the units of work from the National Numeracy Strategy. After the trial the self-assessment sheets were also used with year 5 children.

Bolton Brow Junior and Infant School
Policy on marking in mathematics

Rationale

Marking and feedback should be a positive experience that concentrates on what children can do and helps them to understand any mistakes they have made.

- It is not about giving ticks and totalling marks. This will do nothing for children lacking confidence in mathematics. Furthermore, it will only appeal to the 'egos' of those who are high achievers. Their focus should be on the problem and not their success rate out of 20.

- In general, marking should be done with the children during the lesson. It is not necessary for children or teachers to put a tick against work. When marking their work children should be encouraged to discuss whether they now understand the problem, not whether it was right or wrong when they first did it.

- It is not a good use of teacher time marking away from the children with ticks and totals. It is too time-consuming to write detailed comments on all work each day; indeed, comments are not always understood by the child. However, children's work should be looked at regularly (away from the children) to help with the process of what to do next and to look for any common problems. These should be followed up in the next lesson.

- The aim of marking should be to get children to focus on their work and understand why they have made any mistakes. This should be built into all mathematics lessons.

- If the intention is to set a test for children to see how they perform across areas of mathematics then the marks should be for the teacher and if work is handed back it should be to guide children to understand their mistakes.

- The children can mark oral tests themselves but the total should not be called out. It is better if teachers collect the work and total marks.

Bolton Brow Junior and Infant School
Outline of mathematics assessment

1   Write weekly planner according to sample medium-term plan.

2   In the outcome column of the medium-term plan highlight any groups or individuals that don't achieve objectives.

3   At the end of each unit record achievement on class assessment record. This may have to be done at a later date if there is not enough evidence to fulfil the whole objective.

4   Every one or two weeks test mental work that you have been covering and record marks (more than 15 minutes).

5   Key stage 1 – NTAs could mark work; key stage 2 – children mark work.

6   Each half-term record one 'using and applying' assessment on the record sheet.

7   Each half-term, assess and review the units of work covered. This needs to be built into planning.

8   Discuss with children (usually in groups) their work on this unit.

9   National curriculum test, or similiar test, given every year in May and a level recorded for each child.

10 Classes 2 and 6 given practice national curriculum tests and levels recorded throughout the year.

It must be remembered that just feeding back marks or levels to children may demotivate. It is better to praise what they can do and teach and explain what they have not yet grasped.

Bolton Brow Junior and Infant School
Assessment guidelines

Short-term assessments

- Check children grasped main teaching points.
- Check children remember number facts.
- Make assessments against the learning objectives of the lesson.
- In the outcome column of the weekly planning sheet highlight any groups or individuals that don't achieve the objectives of the lesson. This will help you decide what to do next.
- Use the plenary session to acknowledge individual and collective achievement.

Medium-term assessments

- Review and record progress children are making against the key objectives class sheet.
- To help record progress, group and individual assessment activities and written tasks should be planned at the end of each unit of work. Any difficulties should be rectified as soon as possible and you need to take account of these difficulties in the next phase of medium-term planning.
- Before a unit of work is started you should talk to the children about what they will be learning and refer to their individual self-assessment sheets.
- Every one or two weeks test mental work that you have been covering and record marks.
- All classes should be given opportunities from time to time to complete a range of tests that they have covered for that year.
- Each half-term you should meet with children (mainly groups) to discuss what they have been learning. The children should be given the opportunity to express what they understand and what they have still not grasped. The child self-assessment sheets can be used again this time.
- A few children may need notes keeping about them. These will be children whose work differs markedly from the majority of the class.

Long-term assessments

During key stage 2 national curriculum tests week, all individual children in each class will be assessed.

Passing on assessments to the next class teacher

- Pass on key objectives class sheet.
- Marks collected for mental tests.
- Marks for tests on areas and groups of areas of mathematics.
- Optional or statutory test level.
- Brief discussion about new class between two teachers.

Case study 3:
The Blake School

Background

The Blake School is a secondary school with 575 pupils and is situated on a large council estate in the Somerset town of Bridgwater. Two-thirds of each year group come from the main feeder primary school also situated on the estate and an average of just over 30 per cent of pupils have been achieving level 4+ in mathematics at the end of key stage 2. The results in mathematics GCSE are considerably higher than the average for the school. Fifty per cent of pupils have been achieving grades A* to C in mathematics, compared with the school average of 38 per cent.

This case study shows how clear learning objectives and feedback to pupils can be used to improve pupils' performance.

The learning environment
The mathematics department

In 1994 the philosophy of the mathematics department was directly affected by the low ability intake. From a four-form entry, only the top set and a few from set 2 sat the intermediate level GCSE, of which three or four pupils were entered for the higher tier. The rest of the year group were either entered for the foundation level or followed an individual learning programme leading to modular accreditation at a level below GCSE with little direct teaching taking place. However, the percentage of pupils achieving C or above at GCSE was about 5 per cent higher than other departments in the school.

Establishing high expectations and an effective learning environment

In 1995 a new head of department was appointed and the individual learning programme was immediately abandoned. Set 1 followed the higher level course, sets 2 and 3 the intermediate, and set 4 the foundation. To support teaching, the department purchased a full set of GCSE books for years 10 and 11. The philosophy of the department became 'You can do it' rather than 'They have not got the ability to do it'. The next move was to change the course followed at key stage 3 and to purchase a mathematics scheme for years 7, 8 and 9. The structure of the scheme meant that all sets in effect followed the same pattern of topics but at different levels. This was important to allow pupils to move between sets, for making assessments across a year group or sets and for pupils' self-esteem. The two non-specialists working within the department found the support material with the scheme invaluable.

At the same time new school initiatives were introduced, such as having individual pupil targets. Every pupil in key stage 3 was given a target minimum level in English, mathematics and science and then a target minimum grade for all GCSE subjects. These targets were calculated by using the schools' historic data and the Analysis module on Sims Assessment Manager. Records of achievement as a means of reporting to parents were replaced by a numerical method of reporting different aspects of pupils' work and behaviour, accompanied by specific targets or 'subject next steps'. These were clear statements of advice on what the pupils should do to improve their learning and the level at which they were working.

Target-setting

The teaching approach

With the changes to the department firmly in place, time could now be spent concentrating on teaching and assessment. The teaching strategies were very much in line with those now being implemented via the National Numeracy Strategy. An emphasis was placed on raising each pupil's self-esteem, levels of expectation at GCSE and sharing explicit learning objectives.

Often, pupils' questions involve the 'whys' and 'what-fors' about individual topics. Now information about every aspect of the syllabus was passed on at every stage. Pupils understood what they were to learn, why and where it was leading. Each new topic was introduced by describing the components and where they fitted in to the national curriculum levels. Pupils wrote the relevant levels into their exercise books as well as questions they would be able to complete by the end of the topic.

Pupils were encouraged to think of the syllabus as a large jigsaw puzzle and each chapter as a piece in the puzzle. No topic was seen to be in isolation. When the topic was taught, the work did not stop at a predefined level. So if the work was going well, levels 6 or 7 could be reached even if level 5 was the starting point.

Each lesson followed the same pattern. At the start of each lesson a brief outline of what was going to happen that day was written on the board. One of the most important aspects of which would be a target question, 'This is what is to be solved by the end of the lesson'. Wherever and whenever possible this was to be a question taken from a past GCSE paper. For example, part of year 7's work in the autumn term is coordinates and the development to straight-line graphs. This topic always now concludes with a recent GCSE paper being held up, and the relevant question being written down and successfully completed. Pupils always comment on how easy the questions are, so the process of removing the fear factor of the exams has begun. The year 7 parents' evening in early December invariably includes comments from parents about how excited their child has been to report back to them that a GCSE exam question had been completed easily.

To reinforce the increase in pupils' knowledge of what is taught and where it fits in, a syllabus booklet is given to each pupil, which contains an outline of the year's work. This booklet, which is an adaptation of the contents page of the textbook, also has space for test results to be recorded and targets to be written and is kept inside the cover of their current exercise book.

Assessment and feedback strategies

Tests

New tests were written for all years. There were four different types of test, each for different purposes. These were:

- short topic tests at the end of each chapter. These were built around the tests provided in the textbooks;
- half-termly tests covering the topics taught to date;
- regular mental arithmetic tests;
- the year tests, which coordinate with the school examinations.

The results were recorded in the pupils' syllabus booklet. The teacher commented in the syllabus booklet (in bullet points) on what the pupil needed to do in order to improve their performance.

Self-assessment

One of the biggest headaches for any teacher is the amount of marking to be done. It is impossible to mark everything, so the right balance has to be struck. The major assessments were in place, so a variety of marking methods could be used. Pupils marked the majority of their own work or changed books to mark each other's work for both classwork, such as mental arithmetic tests, and homework. The class teacher collected the books regularly to keep a close eye on the marking and to add the schools' effort and accuracy grades, which were linked to the school's rewarding policy. These grades were on a 5 to 1 scale. By collecting effort and accuracy grades of 4s and 5s, pupils receive credits that will be added to their pupil profile files. No other comment is recorded. This replaces the use of praise in marking, such as 'well done' and 'excellent'. The only comment to be added at any stage is one whereby the teacher informs the pupil of what should be done in order to improve their performance.

This style of feedback is linked to the school's assessment, recording and reporting policy. The school reports to parents three times per year. In November and June an overview is given consisting of pupils' target minimum levels or grades and the levels at which they are currently working. Effort, homework, behaviour, coursework and listening grades are also assessed on a 5 to 1 scale. In February, a work report supplements this. Each department gives an overview of the work completed and a comment under the heading of 'subject next steps'. This involves a statement of what pupils need to do in order to improve the level at which they are presently working.

The GCSE results for The Blake School

The percentage A*–C GCSE results for the past four years are as follows:

	1996	1997	1998	1999	2000
School	18	34	27	30	38
Mathematics department	33	47	43	46	50

Ofsted Inspection Report

An inspection took place from 29 November to 3 December 1999. Main findings listed under what the school does well included:

- 'There are very good arrangements to assess pupils' work and set targets for improvement;'
- 'Pupils are well supported and receive very good guidance to help them in their studies.'

Case study 4:
Churchill Community School

Background

Churchill Community School is a large 11–18 coeducational comprehensive school with 1,720 pupils, including 420 in the sixth form. It serves a 35 square mile catchment area and is situated in the lee of the Mendip Hills in north Somerset, 15 miles south of Bristol and eight miles east of Weston-super-Mare. It has 12 contributory primary schools. The school attracts over a quarter of its total population from Weston-super-Mare by parental choice.

In 2000 the percentage of pupils entitled to free school meals as a proportion of its 11–16 pupil population was 6.8 per cent. Ten per cent of pupils were on the special needs register, of whom 2.5 per cent have statements of special needs.

Performance at key stage 3 is well above the national average in all three core subjects and has been for the past five years. It also performs above the national average in comparison with similar schools (applying the free school meal proxy).

At GCSE 63 per cent of the pupils achieved five or more grades A* to C and the average pupil score was 46.3. At GCE A level the average point score was 20.8.

In its last Ofsted inspection (1997) the school was seen as 'a good school with several very good features including the breadth of the curriculum, its staff development, its music and its particularly strong sixth form'.

Since this inspection the school has made significant progress, fulfilled its action plan and been re-awarded its Investors in People status. It is also making great strides towards becoming a self-evaluating school.

This case study demonstrates how targets can be used to improve performance and how they are identified by formative assessment and self-assessment.

The learning environment

The delivery of mathematics

The school curriculum follows a fortnightly timetable of five 60-minute lessons per day. For each year group lessons are spread over the week and at a variety of times during the day.

In year 7 pupils are taught in mixed ability tutor groups for the whole academic year, and in years 8, 9, 10 and 11 they are taught in sets in two half-year blocks.

A faculty aim is to ensure that the same teacher remains with a class throughout key stage 4 and at post-16. In key stage 3 most pupils experience three different teachers.

Resources and examination boards

Key stage 3	Year 7	Use a published mathematics text, introduced this year for the first time.
	Years 8 and 9	Use a combination of faculty generated and published text resources.
Key stage 4	Years 10 and 11	The majority of pupils follow a GCSE syllabus and each pupil has a text resource. Fewer pupils work below GCSE level.
Post-16	Years 12 and 13	Follow an AS and A level syllabus with appropriate text for each pupil and module.

Establishing effective learning

In January 1999, all heads of faculty met for one day to look at how to raise achievement. It was unanimously agreed that there was a dip in effort, behaviour and attainment in year 8, particularly in middle ability pupils. The classroom code of conduct was revisited and six expectations were agreed common to all subjects.

The mathematics faculty incorporated these into a general expectation sheet for all pupils in the mathematics classroom.

The class teacher checks these expectations at the start of every academic year for all classes in key stages 3 and 4. At this stage broad targets and objectives are set for each group for the year, stressing that what they can achieve is not determined by the set they are in but the level of effort they apply. The mathematics they encounter should not be too easy but will be a development on previous work.

The mathematics faculty views each cohort as potentially different from the previous year. Targets for the work covered from the national curriculum, including the challenge level for a particular class and individual, are decided by making full use of the information listed on the opposite page.

In September teachers have class lists for years 8–11, indicating prior attainment including:

- key stage 2 results (if known);
- key stage 3 results;
- previous report grades/levels;
- target minimum levels or grades; } (see **Target-setting**)
- challenge levels or grades;
- standardised test scores.

Teachers also pass on for each teaching group:

- copies of all previous reports and targets;
- outline of work covered for the class in the previous year, with issues raised;
- any pupil learning issues highlighted by the previous teacher or parents;
- copies of tests, MA1 and information and communication technology (ICT) work, etc.

Year 7 teachers have access to:

- transfer information from primary schools;
- key stage 2 results (if known).

All teachers have access to pupil support details.

The school records report grades, levels, key stage 2 and 3 test results, and standardised test results on assessment management software for all subjects. This enables class lists to be easily generated with relevant information about prior attainment and challenge grades/levels set for individuals. It is worth noting that mathematics and science teachers have found it useful to look at respective attainment. In addition, the mathematics faculty adds onto assessment manager test results and mock results data to the management database.

Target-setting

Target-setting began in key stage 4 in September 1998 and has been adapted and introduced into key stage 3 in the last academic year, starting with year 7. In both key stages it is part of the report-writing process.

Key stage 4

In all subjects pupils are set a target minimum grade and challenge grade for key stage 4. To enable teachers to make such judgements by the end of the autumn term in year 10, teachers use standardised test scores and, in mathematics, national curriculum test results. Class teachers discuss these grades with pupils. The class teacher gives a current attainment grade on all reports. The target minimum grade remains unaltered (unless there are exceptional reasons) throughout key stage 4; it is the challenge and attainment grade that alters.

At the end of the autumn term in year 10 pupils set their own learning targets on an interim report. These targets are discussed and negotiated with the class teacher. To aid the process mathematics teachers use formative assessment from September. The annotation (T) for 'specific target for improvement' is used with a written comment when marking classwork, homework and when evaluating class tests. Teachers do not need to identify a target every time work is looked at; they use it when a learning objective is not being met. This target should not only highlight a weakness but should also try to provide a strategy for improvement where appropriate. Pupils are actively encouraged to review their own work and set themselves targets as an ongoing part of the process. Many pupils find the process of setting their own targets at the end of the autumn term on their interim merely a matter of looking through their exercise books and deciding which targets are still current.

The class teacher comments if the targets have been met in the full report at the end of year 10 and sets new ones for the year 11 report. The process is a continuous one. Many pupils are aware of the targets that their class teacher may set on their next report as the targets will already have been indicated by the teacher or student after a piece of work, test or exam with a (T).

Key stage 3

The target-setting process in key stage 3 begins in the spring term of year 7. Teachers set a target minimum level and challenge level for the end of year 9.

When target-setting was first introduced in 1999/2000 the faculty used meeting time to look at the value added from year 7 to year 9, in terms of national curriculum levels for the year 10 cohort. For example, roughly 60 per cent of the pupils with a key stage 2 level 4 achieved a level 6 at the end of key stage 3. For current key stage 2 level 4 pupils, teachers set a target minimum level of 5 or 6 with a challenge of 6 or 7 respectively. To support this judgement key stage 2 transfer information, standardised test scores (taken by year 7 in the autumn term) and present attainment are used.

As pupils progress through key stage 3 the challenge level is raised if appropriate. The target minimum level and challenge level are given on yearly full reports along with current attainment, which can be a sub-divided national curriculum level. The aim is for pupils to have an idea as to where they are in the process and where they are heading, and to feel challenged.

As with key stage 4 the full reports also require teachers to write targets for improvement and to reflect on those previously set. The mathematics faculty has adopted the same (T) for 'specific target for improvement' to assess pupils' work throughout key stage 3.

Measuring the project's success

Evaluating target-setting

It is difficult to measure the success of target-setting in terms of improved exam results in key stage 4. This is because there has only been one completed cycle to date and there has not been a subset acting as control group. In key stage 3 the first cohort is still in year 8.

Nevertheless, within the mathematics faculty it has enabled the school to do the following:

1 Look at formative assessment in terms of assessment criteria against learning objectives and student involvement.

The use of (T) for 'specific target for improvement' was discussed and agreed at a faculty meeting. It has evolved from being used in the assessment of learning into the school's marking policy as a tool for ongoing *assessment for learning* (see the marking policy on page 49). Although mathematics teachers were comfortable in identifying when and what learning targets should be set, pupils have found this more difficult; it is apparent that they need guidance. Some pupils can be highly critical of their work if they have not answered all the questions correctly. They may, for example, set themselves a target to learn solving equations more thoroughly when in fact they got only a few incorrect and this was due to numerical errors rather than omitting the inverse operation needed. As a result, class teachers have needed to give clear guidelines on the learning objective and assessment criteria that they are looking for. They are realising the potential of using peer assessment as well as teacher evaluation. The beginning of the lessons should set out the learning objectives and key words used.

2 Help teachers plan their lessons and set better learning objects in response to pupils and whole-class needs.

Writing formative targets has contributed towards teachers setting improved learning objectives. Raising the profile of written formative assessment has enabled teachers to be more aware of other methods of assessment and judgements, such as questioning, oral feedback, pupil evaluation or setting structured activities/questions in class and homework that clearly identifies learning objectives by its content. Teachers are responding to common and individual issues identified in terms of future objective-setting in the classroom.

3 Set positive high expectations and challenges for individual and whole classes.
4 Involve pupils in the learning process and encourage responsibility.

Teachers are experiencing an increased sense that pupils are working *with* them rather than *for* them. For example, pupils are asking for more questions or examples to practise applying their understanding of a topic or to repeat homework or tests if they have not met the standard and the objectives that they and the teacher have set.

5 Create a more fluid transition particularly through key stage 3, where pupils are often taught by three teachers.
6 Help the procedure of identifying under-achieving pupils.
7 Better inform parents of their child's progress.

The target-setting and report-writing process has enabled parents and pupils to gain a better understanding of current progress: what has gone well, what needs to be worked on and what could be achieved by the end of a key stage. In addition to post-report parents' evenings there are two whole-school curriculum evenings in the autumn term, one for year 8 and one for year 10. Heads of faculty give a short presentation to highlight the target-setting process and ways to support their child's learning.

8 Self-evaluate.

The faculty uses information gathered from the target-setting process to help monitoring and self-evaluation inform teaching. Last academic year the faculty looked at differentiation in key stage 3. Pupils were interviewed, lessons observed and national curriculum test results were analysed per teaching group and also for value added from key stage 2. The cross-section of pupils interviewed was very positive about the use of (T) in marking; a few remarked how their parents had also viewed it as useful. Those now in year 8 felt better informed about their progress. One pupil remarked enthusiastically, My year 7 report said I could get a challenge level of 7 in year 9, miss. I only got level 4 in year 6.

The use of (T) in marking has merely formalised a process that was already taking place. It has reinforced good practice and is encouraging staff to look at ways of further involving pupils in their own learning and evaluation. The process is enabling the school to look at learning strategies – an integral part of the teacher's role.

Churchill Community School
Marking policy for mathematics faculty

This policy relates to the purpose and practice of ongoing marking of classwork and homework.

Purpose

1 Ongoing marking is to be formative – to help pupils know what they can do, where they are wrong and why, and see ways forward in understanding.

2 Marking should give a clear idea of what pupils have achieved.

3 Marking should encourage pupils and give them confidence to tackle new and more difficult work.

4 Marking should make clear expectations and acknowledge well-presented work.

5 Homework marking in key stage 3 should use the grades and 1 to 4 scale outlined in the school's homework marking scheme. Each pupil should have a copy in their exercise book for reference and evaluation (see page 51).

Practice

Books will be marked by both pupils and the class teacher. When books are seen by the class teacher:

- concise formative comments relating to methodology, accuracy or presentation can be added, and any unmarked work dealt with. The use of (T) as a specific target for improvement should be used where appropriate;
- any pupil marking can be checked at this time;
- teachers should look for any common problems to help with future planning.

Pupils should be encouraged, where practically possible, to take responsibility for marking their own work (just as pupils are encouraged to take responsibility for their learning). Pupils should be encouraged to mark their work or their peers' work accurately and honestly. An opportunity for pupils to evaluate their understanding and acknowledge success in relation to the learning objectives should be encouraged. The degree to which pupils can be expected to mark their own will depend on particular pupils. Teachers will need to use their professional judgement in this issue.

Exercise questions – usually each correct answer should be ticked and an incorrect one crossed. Concise formative comments may also be needed.

Marking investigations and coursework – concise formative comments should be given to highlight strengths and areas where improvements could be made.

Sp	spelling	UC	upper case, capital letter
P	punctuation mark	^	omission
//	new paragraph needed here	/	new sentence needed here
Exp	expression awkward, rephrase	D	dictionary, check meaning of word

Notation – to help concise commenting on investigations and course work the school code should be adopted:

✔	working correct/answer correct	x	work incorrect
?	explanation or working unclear	ims	incorrect mathematical statement, eg 2 x 3 – 6 + 4 = 10
✔	or **ft** follow through	(T)	specific target for improvement

In addition, the following may be useful in marking mathematics:

Spelling – the faculty should concentrate on the correct spelling of mathematical words. Where spelling is not a major difficulty for a pupil, spelling errors should be indicated (see table above) and pupils should be directed to where the correct spelling can be found. For pupil support, occasional help should be given, remembering that encouraging mathematical understanding and skills is the faculty's primary objective. Key mathematical words are usefully displayed on classroom walls. 'Topic of the week' boards with key words and results should be used.

Presentation – work should be dated and have a title. Textbook and worksheet references and questions should be written clearly. Rulers should be used to draw any straight lines. A good standard of neatness should be expected according to the pupil's ability in this area. Where pupils are able to make significant improvements work should be redrafted. Pupils with significant difficulties should be encouraged to use a word processor where one is available. Formulae rules and key words useful for reflection and revision should be highlighted with 'clouds' or boxed off.

Housepoints and positive referrals – these should be awarded in accordance with school and faculty policies in rewards.

Key stage 3 – homework marking scheme

When your homework is marked you should be given two marks: one for mathematics and one for presentation/effort, eg C3.

The following grades and numbers are given with some idea as to how you can achieve them.

Your mathematics

A. Minor errors. All working-out shown.

B. Most working-out shown. Majority Correct.

C. Little working-out shown. Shows some understanding.

D. No working-out shown. Shows little understanding.

Your presentation/effort

1. **Excellent effort**, eg diagrams in pencil using a ruler. Graphics labelled correctly.

2. **Good effort**, eg most diagrams with pencil/ruler, some parts of graph labelled.

3. **Satisfactory effort**, eg diagrams without pencil or ruler.

4. **Poor effort**, eg work not completed.

You may be asked to do poor quality homework again.

Tests results

Test						
Result						

References

Askew, M, & Wiliam, D, *Recent Research in Mathematics Education 5–16 Ofsted Reviews of Research*, HMSO, 1995

Assessment Reform Group, *Assessment for Learning, Beyond the black box*, University of Cambridge School of Education, 1999

Black, P, & Wiliam, D, *Inside the Black Box*, King's College London, 1998

Butler, R, 'Enhancing and Undermining Instrinsic Motivation; the Effects of Task-involving and Ego-involving Evaluation on Interest and Performance' *British Journal of Educational Psychology*, 58, pages 1–14, 1988

Donaldson, M, *Children's Minds*, Fontana Press, 1990

Mitchell, G, and Hirom, K, 'The effect of mentoring on the academic achievement of boys'. Paper presented at the British Educational Research Association annual conference, University of Sussex, 1999

Ofsted, *Teacher assessment in core subjects at key stage 2*, HMSO, 1998

Sadler, R, 'Formative assessment and the design of instructional systems'. *Instructional Science*, 18, pages 119–144, 1998

Weeden, P, & Winter, J, et al 'The LEARN Project: Learners' Expectations of Assessment for Learning Nationally' *University of Bristol, CLIO Centre for Assessment Studies*, Qualifications and Curriculum Authority, 1999

Useful websites and publications

- Assessment for Learning: Summary Sheet
  www.qca.org.uk/ca/5-14/afl/summary_sheet.asp

- Black, P, & Wiliam, D, 'Assessment and Classroom Learning' *Assessment in Education* Vol. 5, No 1, 1998

- Bucks & Oxfordshire LEAs *Target Setting: Using Assessment to Raise Standards,* Oxford County Council, 1999

- Clarke, S, *Targeting Assessment in the Primary Classroom,* Hodder & Stoughton, 1998

- Clio Centre for Assessment Studies, *Developing Assessment in the Primary School,* University of Bristol, 2000
  www.qca.org.uk/pdf.asp?/ca/5-14/afl/developing.pdf

- Effective questioning can raise achievement
  www.standards.dfee.gov.uk/numeracy/prof_dev/?pd=choose
  Subtopic&top_id=428&art_id=3089&preview=0

- James, M, *Using Assessment for (Secondary) School Improvement,* Heinemann, 1998

- McCallum, B, *Formative Assessment, Implications for Classroom Practice,* Institute of Education, 2000
  www.qca.org.uk/pdf.asp?/ca/5-14/afl/formative.pdf

- McGuinness, C, *From thinking skills to thinking classrooms: a review and evaluation of approaches for developing pupils' thinking,* DfEE, 1999

- Neesom, A, *Report of Teachers' Perception of Formative Assessment,* April 2000
  www.qca.org.uk/pdf.asp?/ca/5-14/afl/annneesom.pdf

- Neesom, A, *Teachers use Assessment for Learning to raise standards,* April 2000
  http://www.qca.org.uk/pdf.asp?/ca/5-14/afl/raise.pdf

- Ruddock, J, et al, *Improving Learning: The Pupils' Agenda,* Homerton College Cambridge, 1999

- Sadler, R, *Formative Assessment: revisiting the territory, Assessment in Education* Vol. 5, No 1, 1998

- Weeden, P, Winter, J, & Broadfoot, P, *The LEARN Project Phase 2: Guidance for Schools on Assessment for Learning,* Project Report, 2000
  www.qca.org.uk/pdf.asp?/ca/5-14/afl/guidance.pdf